W9-BLI-858

Big Trucks

Mary Kate Doman

Enslow Elementary

an imprint of

Enslow Publishers, Inc.

40 Industrial Road
Box 398
Berkeley Heights, NJ 07922
USA

http://www.enslow.com

For Liam, who loves things that go.

Enslow Elementary, an imprint of Enslow Publishers, Inc.

Enslow Elementary® is a registered trademark of Enslow Publishers, Inc.

Library of Congress Cataloging-in-Publication Data

Doman, Mary Kate, 1979–
  Big trucks / by Mary Kate Doman.
      p. cm. — (All about big machines)
  Includes index.
  Summary: "Learn how trucks are used every day"—Provided by publisher.
  ISBN 978-0-7660-3929-2
  1. Trucks—Juvenile literature. I. Title.
  TL230.15.D65 2012
  629.224—dc23

                          2011014636

Paperback ISBN 978-1-59845-241-9

052011 Lake Book Manufacturing, Inc., Melrose Park, IL

10 9 8 7 6 5 4 3 2 1

To Our Readers: We have done our best to make sure all Internet Addresses in this book were active and appropriate when we went to press. However, the author and the publisher have no control over and assume no liability for the material available on those Internet sites or on other Web sites they may link to. Any comments or suggestions can be sent by e-mail to comments@enslow.com or to the address on the back cover.

Photo Credits: © 2011 Photos.com, a division of Getty Images. All rights reserved, pp. title page, 6–7, 8–9, 10–11, 18–19, 22; Gary Blakeley / Shutterstock.com, pp. 14–15; Keltr / Shutterstock.com, pp. 16–17; olly / Shutterstock.com, pp. 4–5; Sergey Kozoderov / Shutterstock.com, pp. 12–13; Vibrant Image Studio, pp. 20–21.

Cover Photo: © 2011 Photos.com, a division of Getty Images. All rights reserved.

Note to Parents and Teachers

Help pre-readers get a jumpstart on reading. These lively stories introduce simple concepts with repetition of words and short simple sentences. Photos and illustrations fill the pages with color and effectively enhance the text. Free Educator Guides are available for this series at www.enslow.com. Search for the *All About Big Machines* series name.

Contents

Words to Know

construction   trash   yellow

Big trucks do big jobs.

Big red trucks and big blue trucks do big jobs.

Big trucks do big jobs at construction sites.

Big trucks carry boxes.

Big trucks carry trash.

13

Big yellow trucks
and big green trucks
do big jobs too.

Big trucks do big jobs on farms.

Big trucks carry logs.

Big trucks can even carry cars.

Big trucks do a lot
of big jobs.

Read More

Castor, Harriet and Sean Wilkinson. *Trucks*. London: Usborne Books, 2004.

Ransom, Candice. *Big Rigs*. Minneapolis, Minn: Lerner Publications Company, 2005.

Simon, Seymour. *Seymour Simon's Book of Trucks*. New York: HarperCollins, 2002.

Web Sites

Enchanted Learning: Transportation
<http://www.enchantedlearning.com/themes/ transportation.shtml>

Play the A to Z Highway Game
http://www.randomhouse.com/kids/arthur/truckgame/

Index

Guided Reading Level: C
Guided Reading Leveling System is based on the guidelines recommended by Fountas and Pinnell.

Word Count: 67